P9-BAT-250

THE
LITTLE
GOO-ROO

LESSONS FROM YOUR BABY

- written by -
Jan & Tracy Kirschner
- illustrated by -
Alana Lea Gordey

ATLAS PRESS

Published by

ATLAS PRESS
P.O. Box 7054
Boulder, CO 80306-7054

(303) 546-6529

Text © 1997 Jan & Tracy Kirschner
Illustrations & Typographics © 1997 Alana Lea Gordey

ALL RIGHTS RESERVED

For information about permission to reproduce
selections from this book, please contact the publisher.

ISBN 0-9657960-1-9
Library of Congress Card Catalogue: 97-93617
Book Jacket and Book Design by Alana Lea Gordey
Printed in China

First Printing 1997

- DEDICATED TO -

Naomi and Aaron

- ACKNOWLEDGEMENTS -

- THANKS TO -

- Our families, for teaching us to search for the highest values in life

- Mitch and Laurie Santell, Mary Jo Murawski, Judith Crop, Fred and Debra Poneman, Barry Spilchuk, Valerie Gill and Paul Gilman for their belief in this project

- Gaile Sickel for seeing the match made in heaven

- Clarissa Lackman, residing in heaven, whose bravery and radiance in the face of multiple health challenges was the original inspiration for THE LITTLE GOO-ROO

- Special thanks to all THE LITTLE GOO-ROOS who are pictured giving their verbal instructions:

- Morgan Dale Baillie - Nathan Paul Harte

- Naomi Rose Kirschner - Gavinder Kishan Singh Manhas

- Ruby Leala Rose Smith - Sylvan Tobias Swierkosz

- Tashi Amrita Serena Swierkosz

    AND FINALLY, TO

- Donald Epstein and Jackie Knowles, there at the birth of the title, and at every step of the way since

- INTRODUCTION -

Each of the lessons in this book was learned from our initial experience of the miracles of parenting. We had spent many hours reading numerous books about how to "raise" Naomi; however, we very quickly discovered that it was she who was raising us, literally lifting us higher in our appreciation of life and all of its wonders. Each day with her continues to be an adventure in the miraculous.

You will notice that each page contains one lesson. The facing page is for you to describe how you learned this lesson, or a similar one, from your own "LITTLE GOO-ROO." By observing and writing down your experiences, you will be empowered to use them for your own inner development, and by fully appreciating your child as a teacher, you will create the gratitude and joy necessary to enable you to return these lessons to your children later in life.

For those who are not yet parents, it is our hope that this book will inspire you to bring new life into this world, so much in need of love and healing.

Jan and Tracy Kirschner

ONCE UPON A TIME …

*there were two seekers of truth,
named Jan and Tracy.*

*When they were ready,
their teacher appeared.*

She was THE LITTLE GOO-ROO.

Like most spiritual masters,
THE LITTLE GOO-ROO spent
many months in a dark cave,
all by herself.

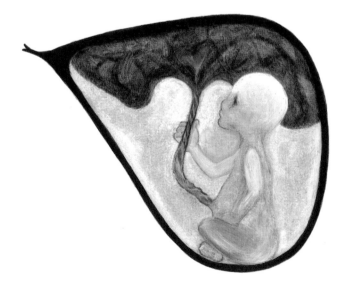

Her students waited for her
with great anticipation.

She waited until
the time was right,
and then revealed herself
to the world.

The name of
THE LITTLE GOO-ROO
was
Na-ommmmm-ee.

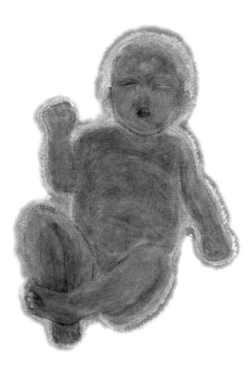

As soon as they saw her
shining face and eyes,
so totally alive and alert,
Tracy and Jan knew that
THE LITTLE GOO-ROO
was meant to be their teacher.

They set about
learning the lessons
she was teaching them
as quickly as they could.

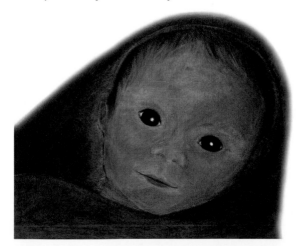

The first lessons
she gave them
were non-verbal,
although often not silent.

When they began
to understand these,
she soon began to issue
verbal instructions,
as well.

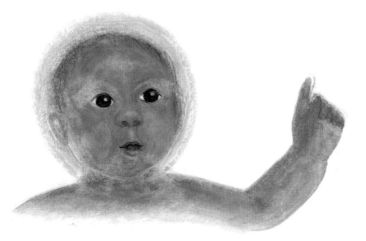

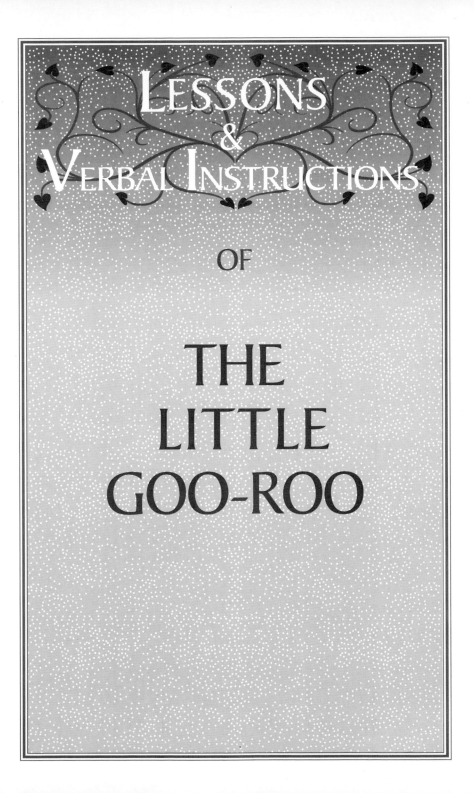

LESSONS
& VERBAL INSTRUCTIONS

OF

THE
LITTLE
GOO-ROO

NOTES

THE SIMPLICITY OF LIFE

For *THE LITTLE GOO-ROO,*
life's activities were
as simple as possible,
leaving most of the day
free for contemplation.

Her students often got lost
in unnecessary complications
in their own lives.

NOTES

UNDIVIDED ATTENTION

When they would become
distracted by the
trivial details of life,
THE LITTLE GOO-ROO
would swiftly remind them
where their attention
needed to be.

This was a very hard lesson.

NOTES

the unimportance of SLEEP

THE LITTLE GOO-ROO
would play tricks on them
in the middle of the night,
so that they would
understand that tiredness
is just an illusion,
a trick of the mind.

NOTES

THE NECESSITY OF TRANQUILITY

Each time the students
got upset with life,
THE LITTLE GOO-ROO
mirrored their distress.

When they were calm,
the teacher soon returned
to her natural, blissful state.

NOTES

EQUANIMITY
TOWARD
BODILY FLUIDS

Much to their surprise,
the students of the GOO-ROO
found that formerly offensive
odors and textures
became simply another
part of life at which
to express wonder.

NOTES

CHANTING TO THE GOO-ROO

The GOO-ROO was always
most pleased whenever
song filled the air,
particularly songs of devotion-
to her.

She was happiest when
these songs were sung
over, and over, and over,
and over, and over...

Her students saw that
they could use...

NOTES

REPETITIVE ACTIVITY
as a means for
SPIRITUAL GROWTH

Diaper, diaper, diaper, feed,
burp, carry, diaper, diaper,
diaper, feed, burp, feed, burp,
carry, diaper, diaper, diaper,
feed, burp, feed, burp, carry,
sing.

NOTES

SEEING THE MIRACULOUS IN ALL EXISTENCE

Once they could perceive
a big pile of poop as
a miracle,
the rest of life became
much easier.

NOTES

PRECISION AS PART OF SPIRITUAL PRACTICE

If they would hold her
in a way that was even
one inch from the desired
position,
she would instruct them
to do it again,
until they got it just right.

- photo -

"Gloo"

Her first verbal instruction.

*"All things in the universe
are connected
and held together."*

NOTES

PATIENCE

Sometimes, she would
withhold a burp
for an hour,
just to see if they
would have the discipline
to continue the task
to completion.

If they failed,
she would make her
displeasure quite clear.

NOTES

STAMINA

THE LITTLE GOO-ROO
would test their ability
to stay focused,
always choosing a time
seemingly at random,
but guaranteed to be
the least convenient
for the fulfillment
of their personal desires.

NOTES

the foolishness of PERSONAL DESIRES

In passing her tests
of stamina,
the students realized
that many of their desires
were, in fact, simply illusions,
and they were actually
much more content
serving THE LITTLE GOO-ROO.

NOTES

HUMILITY

At times,
THE LITTLE GOO-ROO
refused to look at them,
turning her gaze instead
to a spot on the wall,
or over their heads,
seeming to peer into the infinite.

They realized that there are
more interesting things
for a GOO-ROO to do
than play with her students.

NOTES

don't take things PERSONALLY

They began to see that there
were times
when *THE LITTLE GOO-ROO*
needed to cry
no matter what they did.

This helped them
in not taking responsibility
for things in their lives
over which
they had no effect.

.

- 51 -

NOTES

beginner's MIND

Watching *THE LITTLE GOO-ROO*
made them remember
how important it is
to approach each moment
as if it is a new experience.

(It really is, you know!)

- photo -

"Baah"

"Don't be a sheep.
Question all answers,
except those of
THE LITTLE GOO-ROO."

NOTES

TRUE LOVE EXPANDS

The love that they had

for THE LITTLE GOO-ROO

began to translate

more and more

to all creatures,

big and small.

NOTES

COMPASSION

It hurt them so much
when something would
happen to cause
THE LITTLE GOO-ROO
to suffer.

This led them to
a deeper feeling towards all
who were suffering.

NOTES

GRACE OF THE GOO-ROO

Her smile could melt their hearts,
melt the heart of anyone
she met.

They began to look for
their hearts to melt
when meeting anyone,
whether known or unknown.

- photo -

"Hay"

"Let's have a party!
The first milk's
on me!"

NOTES

raising a Joyous NOISE

THE LITTLE GOO-ROO
would recline on her throne,
squealing with great delight
for no apparent reason, other than
the experience of being alive.

It reminded them not to take
their own existence
so seriously.

NOTES

the IMPORTANCE of ACCEPTING the HELP of **B**someone **IGGER**

The comfort and joy that
THE LITTLE GOO-ROO got
from being held by them
reminded them that
they, too, were being
supported by someone,
or something bigger
in the universe.

- photo -

"Boo"

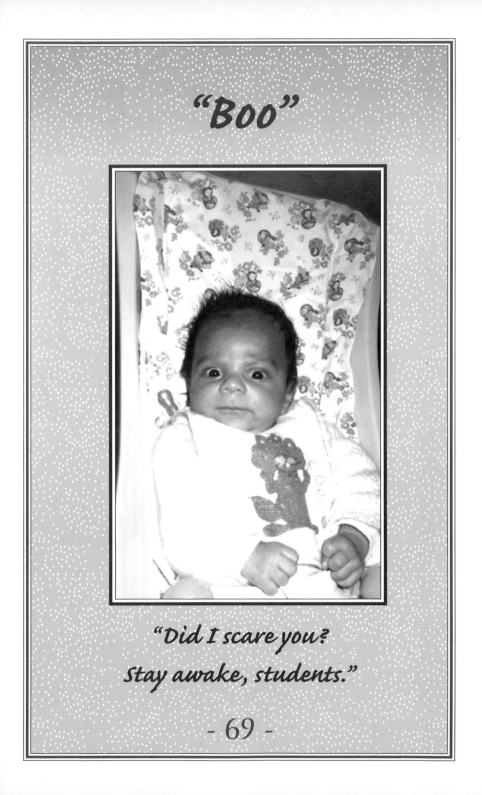

"Did I scare you?
Stay awake, students."

NOTES

the little things MATTER MOST

A simple meal, a good burp,
a smiling face, a loving touch,
an empty diaper...
how easy life seems
when looked at from
the perspective of
THE LITTLE GOO-ROO.

NOTES

ASKING FOR HELP
when you need it

THE LITTLE GOO-ROO
had no false pride,
always getting aid
when she was unable
to do something herself.

They saw that there was
no shame in it,
in fact, it gave great joy
to those who could help out.

- photo -

"Glee"

THE LITTLE GOO-ROO's
comment on the basic
blissful nature
of existence.

NOTES

PROPER
dietary intake

THE LITTLE GOO-ROO
was living proof
that certain foods,
when ingested,
would lead to
unpleasant emotions.

Her students became
more aware
of how what they ate
affected them, as well.

NOTES

PRESENT TIME CONSCIOUSNESS

THE LITTLE GOO-ROO
was completely alive
every single moment,
fully committing to eating,
observing, playing and sleeping.

They saw that they often
went through the motions
in their own lives.

NOTES

Playfulness

Being with
THE LITTLE GOO-ROO
reminded them that
the spirit of joy and play
needed to be alive
in all aspects of their lives.

- photo -

"Doo"

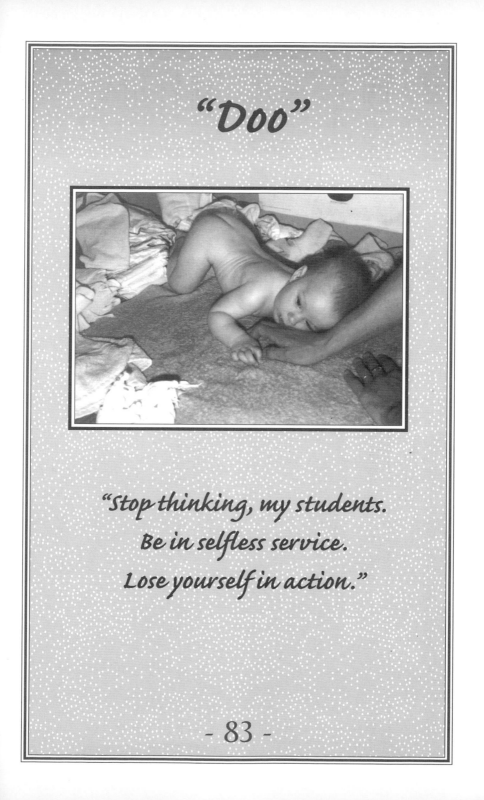

"Stop thinking, my students.
Be in selfless service.
Lose yourself in action."

NOTES

ENJOY THE PROCESS

THE LITTLE GOO-ROO
had no particular agenda,
and yet,
just through the process
of being,
she accomplished all she needed to
in her growth.

They began to be
less attached to results.

NOTES

CHANGE IS INEVITABLE

Every few hours,
change the diaper.

- photo -

"Hi"

Her universal greeting
to all she encountered,
reminding them to
keep their thoughts
and deeds
of the highest quality.

NOTES

comfort
is found
WITHIN

THE LITTLE GOO-ROO
*would sometimes begin to cry,
and then swiftly find her thumb,
and be quieted and delighted.*

NOTES

CURSING
DOESN'T HELP

Language that they had been used to
employing without thinking
was soon seen to be
inappropriate
around one as wise as
THE LITTLE GOO-ROO.

They began to eliminate
those words
throughout their lives.

NOTES

TAKE NOTHING FOR GRANTED

Whenever they thought that
they finally understood
THE LITTLE GOO-ROO's
daily schedule,
she would change it,
just to keep them
fully awake.

- photo -

"Wah-lee"

"Can we watch a re-run of
'Leave it to Beaver?'"

(At least, that's what they
thought she meant.)

NOTES

SURRENDER

They watched *THE LITTLE GOO-ROO*
struggle to keep her eyes open,
and finally give in to sleep.

It was during the struggle
that she seemed most agitated.

Surrender
always brought
peace.

NOTES

HOLD ON TIGHT LET GO LIGHT

THE LITTLE GOO-ROO

would grasp anything within reach,
learn all there was to know
about the object, and gently let go.

They realized that they
were usually more attached
than that to people and
worldly possessions,
grasping them tightly,
but not fully understanding them.

NOTES

Hold your Head up

Almost immediately,
THE LITTLE GOO-ROO
began to work at
holding her head up,
until it was her automatic
way of looking at the world.

Many times, they had
gone through life
with their heads down,
and their eyes not focused
on the present.

- photo -

"Hah"

*"These students
are so amusing me."*

NOTES

keep LEARNING

Each day,
THE LITTLE GOO-ROO
would add to the
things she knew,
and the things
she could do.

They saw that
learning never ends.

NOTES

DON'T Quit

THE LITTLE GOO-ROO
would continue to work
on a new project
until she mastered it.

She would sometimes
get frustrated,
but she would never quit.

NOTES

crawl
before you
WALK

THE LITTLE GOO-ROO
never skipped steps
on her path,
always first mastering
a simpler task,
and then using that skill
to learn something
more complex.

NOTES

Anger

The students began to see
that any hostility or
frustration they felt
impeded THE LITTLE GOO-ROO
in her mission.

They began to surrender
their anger.

- photo -

"How-i-eee?"

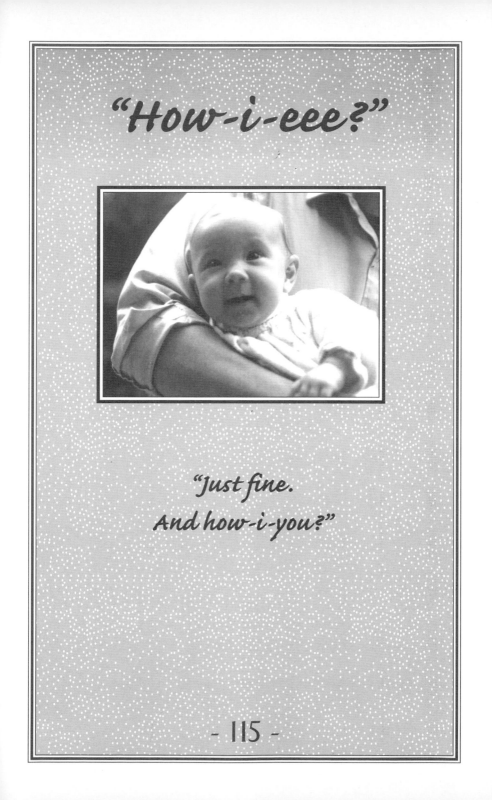

"Just fine.
And how-i-you?"

NOTES

DISCIPLINE

THE LITTLE GOO-ROO
was always either
in action,
in contemplation,
or asleep.

It inspired them to make
each moment
of their lives count.

NOTES

How To
Wake Up

From the first moment of each day,
THE LITTLE GOO-ROO
was fully awake
with a look of gratitude
and delight on her face.

Sometimes, it took
her students hours
to have that look.

Sometimes, it took days.

NOTES

BLESS THE ONES YOU LOVE

THE LITTLE GOO-ROO
always saved her best smile
for those she loved.

For THE LITTLE GOO-ROO,
that was almost everyone she met.

Her students resolved
to emulate the GOO-ROO.

NOTES

Don't Make Plans

Often, when they would
try to set aside
some time
for their own pleasures,
THE LITTLE GOO-ROO
would have other ideas
as to how that time
should best be filled.

They saw that
the universe
works that way, too.

NOTES

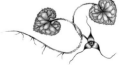

CONTROL

THE LITTLE GOO-ROO
constantly reminded them
that they really had
no control
over most things in
the universe...
except their responses
to it.

NOTES

GROWTH is not always comfortable

THE LITTLE GOO-ROO
experienced a great deal of pain
while teething,
and yet, would rather
have the teeth than not
feel the pain.

They saw that they often
stayed in their comfort
zones, rather than stretch
to new heights in their lives.

NOTES

unconditional
LOVE

THE LITTLE GOO-ROO
held back nothing
in her loving,
and was able to do so
because she had
no judgment of others.

The same could not quite
be said of her students.

- photo -

"Nye"

"Good night, dear students."

Sweet dreams.
And always remember...

NOTES

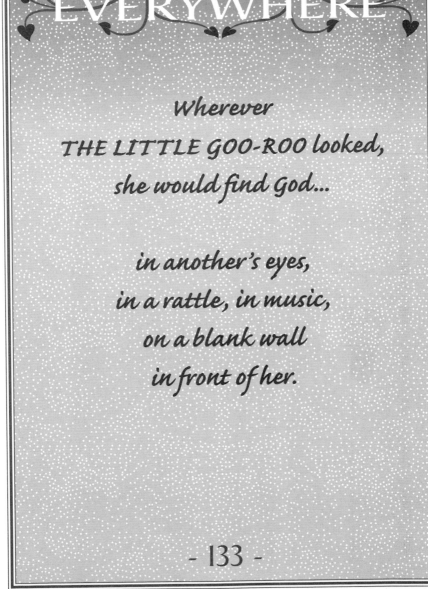

GOD IS EVERYWHERE

Wherever
THE LITTLE GOO-ROO looked,
she would find God...

in another's eyes,
in a rattle, in music,
on a blank wall
in front of her.

- 133 -

NOTES

Her students began to
trust that her vision
was the accurate one,
and that this was
the greatest lesson
of all.

- AFTERWORD -

- Use the journal pages of this book to record additional lessons that you learn from your "Goo-Roo".

- Paste in photos that reflect your experiences.

- Send copies of your own lessons to the publisher of this book, for possible in-clusion in the next volume in this series, "MORE LITTLE GOO-ROOS".

We look forward to hearing from you in our shared journey of parenthood.

- INDEX OF THE LESSONS -

- INDEX OF THE LESSONS -

- INDEX OF VERBAL INSTRUCTIONS -

- BOOK ORDERS -

To order additional copies of "THE LITTLE GOO-ROO"

Phone: (888) 546-6520 (toll-free) OR (303) 546-6529
Fax: (303) 413-1413   Email: litgooroo @ aol.com
    OR
Mail your order to:
Atlas Press, P.O.Box 7054, Boulder. CO 80306-7054

PLEASE SUPPLY THE FOLLOWING INFORMATION:

- Total number of Books ordered
    - $16.95 U.S. / $21.95 Canadian each, plus shipping

- Name, Address, City, State, Zip, and Telephone of each recipient

- Payment Method:
    - Check, Visa, MasterCard, Discover
        - Name on Card, Card number, Expiration date
    Mail or Fax orders, please include:
        - Signature of Card holder

- Shipping Method:
    - Air mail: $3.50 per book within the U.S.A.
    - Book rate: $2.00 for the first book,
            $. 75 each additional book
    Surface shipping may take three to four weeks

- Sales Tax:
    - Please add local sales tax for books shipped to
      Colorado addresses

- - -

You may return unmarked books for a full refund, for any
reason, no questions asked, within thirty days of purchase.